Introduction

This comprehensive guide demystifies the home buying process, offering readers a step-by-step journey from the initial contemplation of purchasing a home to the exhilaration of settling into a new community. It covers essential topics such as understanding your housing needs, navigating financial preparation, choosing the right mortgage, and mastering the art of negotiation. The guide also delves into the closing process, moving logistics, and the responsibilities of homeownership, providing practical advice for maintaining your home and engaging with your new community. Designed for first-time buyers and seasoned homeowners alike, this book serves as a roadmap to making informed decisions, ensuring a smooth transition, and embracing the joys and challenges of homeownership. It's an indispensable resource for anyone looking to turn the dream of owning a home into reality, fostering a sense of confidence and preparedness as they embark on this significant life milestone.

Overview of the Home Buying Process

Purchasing a home is often seen as a hallmark of personal and financial achievement, a process brimming with emotions ranging from excitement to anxiety. It's a journey that involves more than just selecting a house and making a payment; it's about finding a place where you'll create memories, grow, and perhaps even start a family. However, navigating the path to homeownership can be complex and fraught with challenges. This guide aims to illuminate the path, providing you with the knowledge and confidence needed to make informed decisions every step of the way.

Importance of Being Prepared

Entering the home buying process well-prepared can significantly reduce stress and help avoid common pitfalls. Preparation involves understanding your financial situation, knowing what you want in a home, and familiarizing yourself with the steps and decisions you'll face. This book will guide you through financial preparations, choosing the right home, negotiating deals, and finally, closing on your new home.

What to Expect from This Guide

"The Homebuyer's Journey" is structured to follow the sequential steps of buying a home, from the initial stages of understanding your needs and financial preparation to the exciting moment of moving into your new home. Each chapter delves into critical aspects of the process, offering practical advice, strategies, and tips to help you navigate the complex world of real estate with ease. Whether you're a first-time buyer or looking to purchase your next home, this guide is designed to provide you with a comprehensive overview of the journey to homeownership.

Chapter 1
Understanding Your Needs

Assessing Your Long-Term Goals

Before embarking on your home search, it's crucial to consider what you want in the long term. Are you looking for a starter home you'll stay in for a few years, or are you searching for a forever home where you'll spend many decades? Your long-term goals will influence the type of property you buy, its location, size, and even the kind of mortgage you might choose. Take the time to reflect on your career plans, family planning, and lifestyle preferences as they will significantly impact your decision.

Reflect on Your Lifestyle Goals

Family Planning: Consider whether you plan to start or expand your family. The size and layout of your home, as well as its location, should accommodate your current and future family needs.

Career Aspirations: Think about your career path and how stable your job is. Will you need to relocate for work opportunities? Your home's location and flexibility to sell or rent it out should align with your career plans.

Retirement Plans: If you're buying a home later in life, consider how the property fits into your retirement plans. Accessibility, maintenance, and proximity to healthcare services can be crucial factors.

Evaluate Financial Objectives

Investment Perspective: Determine if you're viewing the home primarily as an investment or as a place to live and grow. This perspective will influence the type of property you buy and its location.

Equity Building: Think about how owning a home fits into your wealth-building strategy. Consider how much you can afford to put down and how the mortgage payments will affect your ability to save for other goals.

Long-Term Affordability: Project your future income and expenses to ensure you can comfortably afford the home over the long term, especially as your financial situation changes.

Consider Lifestyle Preferences and Flexibility

Hobbies and Interests: Your home should facilitate the lifestyle you desire, whether that means having space for hobbies, a home office, or proximity to outdoor activities.

Social and Community Needs: Reflect on the importance of being near friends, family, or specific types of communities. Your sense of belonging can significantly impact your satisfaction with your home.

Flexibility for Change: Life can be unpredictable. Consider how easy it would be to sell the home or adapt it to future needs if your circumstances change.

Making a Plan

Set Priorities: Once you've assessed your goals, prioritize them. Knowing what's most important to you will help guide your home buying decisions.

Consult with Professionals: Financial advisors and real estate agents can provide valuable insights and help you align your home buying choices with your long-term goals.

Revisit and Adjust: Your goals may evolve, so revisit them periodically and be prepared to adjust your plans as necessary.

Assessing your long-term goals before buying a home ensures that your purchase supports your broader life plans. This thoughtful approach helps you make informed decisions, leading to greater satisfaction and financial stability in the long run. Whether you're looking for a forever home, a stepping stone property, or an investment, aligning your purchase with your long-term objectives is key to achieving your dreams.

The Significance of Location and Community

The old adage "location, location, location" holds true when buying a home. A house that fits your needs but is in an undesirable location may not be the dream home you envision. Consider factors such as proximity to work, quality of local schools, access to amenities, public transportation options, and the overall feel of the community. Researching and visiting potential neighborhoods at different times of the day and week can provide valuable insights into the area's dynamics.

Evaluating Location

Proximity to Work: Consider the distance and time it takes to commute to your workplace. A shorter commute can significantly enhance your quality of life by reducing travel time and stress.

Access to Schools: For families with children, the quality and proximity of local schools are paramount. Research school districts and specific schools within your target neighborhoods to ensure they meet your educational standards.

Safety and Crime Rates: Investigate the safety of potential neighborhoods. Online crime maps and local police reports can provide insights into the area's safety.

Local Amenities: Evaluate the availability of essential amenities such as grocery stores, hospitals, parks, and recreational facilities. Easy access to these services adds convenience and enjoyment to your daily life.

Public Transportation: If you rely on public transport, consider how well the area is served by buses, trains, or subways. Good public transportation links can also positively affect property values.

Future Development: Look into any planned developments or zoning changes in the area that might affect your living environment and the future value of the property.

Understanding Community

Neighborhood Dynamics: Spend time in the community at different times of the day and week to get a feel for the neighborhood's vibe and dynamics. Are the streets quiet or lively? Do residents take pride in their homes and gardens?

Community Engagement: Research if the neighborhood has active community groups, associations, or social clubs that align with your interests. A strong sense of community can significantly enhance your living experience.

Cultural and Recreational Activities: Consider what cultural, recreational, or social activities are available. Communities with theaters, museums, sports leagues, and public events offer enriching ways to spend your free time.

Demographics: Look into the demographics of the area to ensure it aligns with your preferences. You might be looking for a family-friendly neighborhood, a vibrant young professionals' scene, or a quiet retirement community.

Environmental Concerns: Assess any environmental issues or concerns in the area, such as flood risks or pollution levels. Environmental factors can impact both your quality of life and insurance costs.

Making the Decision

List Your Priorities: After evaluating various factors, list what's most important to you and your family regarding location and community. This list will guide your home search and help you make compromises if necessary.

Consider Long-Term Value: A great location can protect your investment and potentially lead to higher resale value in the future. Consider the long-term prospects of the neighborhood.

Visit and Revisit: Spend as much time as possible in the neighborhoods you're considering. Talk to locals, visit local businesses, and try to envision your daily life in each community.

Choosing the right location and community is about finding a balance between your needs, lifestyle preferences, and budget. The right community can offer not just a place to live, but a place to belong and thrive. Remember, while houses can be altered and renovated, the location and the essence of the community is the constants that will shape your experience of home.

Chapter 2
Financial Preparation

Overview of Budgeting for a Home Purchase

The first step in financial preparation is establishing a realistic budget that accounts for the total cost of homeownership. This includes the purchase price, closing costs, moving expenses, and ongoing maintenance. Understanding your financial situation is crucial-consider your income, debts, and other financial obligations. Tools like mortgage calculators can help you estimate monthly payments and how much house you can afford based on your income and debt.

Understanding Total Homeownership Costs

Purchasing a home involves a variety of costs beyond the down payment and monthly mortgage payments. Prospective homeowners need to account for:

Closing Costs: Typically, 2-5% of the home's purchase price, covering fees for the loan, title transfer, legal services, inspections, and appraisals.
Moving Expenses: The cost of moving can vary widely depending on the distance, amount of belongings, and whether you hire professional movers or do it yourself.
Home Maintenance and Repairs: Setting aside 1-3% of the home's purchase price annually for maintenance and unexpected repairs is a prudent strategy.
Property Taxes and Home Insurance: Often included in mortgage payments if escrowed, but important to budget for these recurring expenses separately if not.

Setting a Realistic Budget

A realistic budget is grounded in your monthly income, expenses, and savings goals. It's essential to:

Analyze Your Spending: Track your spending to understand where your money goes each month and identify areas for potential savings.

Determine Your Affordability: Use mortgage calculators to estimate how much house you can afford based on your income, debt, and the current interest rate.

Factor in Lifestyle Changes: Consider how your lifestyle might change with homeownership, such as increased commuting costs, and adjust your budget accordingly.

Saving Strategies

Saving for a home requires discipline and sometimes creative strategies:

Automatic Savings: Set up automatic transfers to a dedicated savings account for your down payment and home-related expenses.

Reduce Expenses: Identify non-essential expenses you can reduce or eliminate, such as dining out, subscription services, and luxury items.

Increase Income: Consider ways to increase your income through side hustles, overtime work, or pursuing higher-paying job opportunities.

Managing Expenses After Purchase

Once you've purchased your home, managing your expenses becomes crucial to maintaining financial stability:

Emergency Fund: Aim to have an emergency fund of 3-6 months' worth of living expenses, which can be a lifeline in the case of unexpected repairs or job loss.

Regular Maintenance: Regular home maintenance can prevent more costly repairs down the line. Plan and budget for these ongoing costs.

Prioritize Improvements: For non-essential home improvements, prioritize based on need, value added, and your current financial situation.

Understanding and Improving Your Credit Score

Your credit score plays a significant role in determining the mortgage terms available to you, including interest rates. A higher credit score can lead to more favorable loan conditions. This section will explain how credit scores are calculated, why they matter, and strategies to improve your score, such as paying down debt, correcting errors on your credit report, and avoiding new credit inquiries in the months leading up to your home purchase.

How Credit Scores Are Calculated

Credit scores are numerical representations of your creditworthiness, based on your credit history. The most common model, FICO, ranges from 300 to 850 and is calculated using five main factors:

Payment History (35%): Your record of paying bills on time is the most significant factor. Late payments, foreclosures, bankruptcies, and collections can negatively impact your score.

Amounts Owed (30%): This is also known as your credit utilization ratio, which is the amount of credit you're using compared to your total available credit. Lower ratios are seen as indicative of responsible credit use.

Length of Credit History (15%): Longer credit histories are generally viewed more favorably, as they provide more data on your borrowing behavior.

New Credit (10%): Opening several credit accounts in a short period can be seen as risky, especially for people without a long credit history.

Types of Credit in Use (10%): Having a mix of account types (e.g., credit cards, mortgage, auto loans) can be beneficial, though it's not as critical as other factors.

Why Your Credit Score Matters in Home Buying

Your credit score affects your ability to secure a mortgage and the terms of your loan:

Loan Approval: Lenders use credit scores to assess the risk of lending money. Higher scores make it easier to get approved for a mortgage.

Interest Rates: Your credit score directly influences the interest rate you're offered. A higher score can lead to significantly lower rates, saving you thousands over the life of your loan.

Strategies for Improving Your Credit Score

Improving your credit score can take time, but the financial benefits are worth the effort:

Pay Bills on Time: Set up payment reminders or automatic payments to ensure you never miss a bill, as your payment history has the most significant impact on your score.

Reduce Debt: Aim to keep your credit utilization ratio under 30%. Pay down balances, and avoid closing unused credit cards, as this can increase your ratio.

Avoid New Credit Applications: Each application can cause a small, temporary drop in your score. Only apply for new credit if necessary.

Regularly Check Your Credit Report: Errors on your credit report can affect your score. You're entitled to a free report from each of the three major credit bureaus once a year. Dispute any inaccuracies to have them removed.

Be Patient: Rebuilding credit takes time. Consistent, responsible credit behavior is key to improving your score over time.

Saving for a Down Payment

The down payment is often the most substantial upfront cost in buying a home. Traditional mortgages usually require a down payment ranging from 5% to 20% of the home's purchase price. However, there are various loan programs available that may allow for lower down payments, especially for first-time homebuyers. This section will discuss saving strategies, the pros and cons of a larger versus smaller down payment, and how to find and qualify for down payment assistance programs.

Automate Your Savings

Automating your savings can simplify the process and help ensure consistency. Here's how to leverage it effectively:

Direct Deposit Allocations: If your employer offers direct deposit, allocate a specific portion of your paycheck to go directly into a savings account dedicated to your home purchase.

Scheduled Transfers: Use your bank's online banking platform to set up automatic transfers from your checking account to your savings account right after each payday.

Reduce High-Interest Debt

High-interest debt, like credit card balances, can significantly hinder your ability to save by eating into your monthly budget with interest payments.

Debt Snowball or Avalanche Methods: Consider using the debt snowball (paying off debts from smallest to largest balance) or debt avalanche (paying off debts by interest rate, highest to lowest) methods to reduce and eventually eliminate high-interest debt.

Balance Transfer Credit Cards: If you have high credit card balances, transferring the balance to a card with a lower interest rate can reduce the amount of interest you pay each month, freeing up more money for savings.

Adjust Your Budget

A detailed review and adjustment of your budget can reveal opportunities to save more aggressively.

Cut Non-Essential Expenses: Review your monthly expenses and identify areas where you can cut back, such as dining out, subscriptions you don't use, or luxury services.

Downgrade Services: Look for less expensive alternatives for necessary services, like insurance, phone plans, or even rent, if downsizing for a short period is feasible.

Increase Your Income

Boosting your income can significantly impact your savings rate.

Ask for a Raise or Seek Higher-Paying Employment: Evaluate your current earnings and consider if seeking a raise or looking for a new job could substantially increase your income.

Side Hustles: Engaging in a side hustle can provide extra income specifically for your home savings. Choose something that fits your skill set and schedule.

Save Windfalls

Any unexpected or additional income should go directly into your savings.

Tax Refunds, Bonuses, and Gifts: Commit to depositing any windfalls, such as tax refunds, work bonuses, or monetary gifts, into your home savings account.

Sell Unwanted Items: Selling items you no longer need or use can provide a boost to your savings. Online marketplaces make it easier than ever to sell goods.

Prioritize Your Savings Goals

When saving for a home, it's important to prioritize this goal above others.

Reevaluate Short-Term Spending Goals: Delaying gratification on big purchases or vacations can redirect substantial funds towards your down payment.

Set Milestones: Break down your savings goal into smaller, manageable milestones to maintain motivation and track progress.

Getting Pre-approved for a Mortgage

Obtaining a mortgage pre-approval is a critical step in the home buying process. It not only gives you an idea of what you can afford but also signals to sellers that you are a serious and prepared buyer. This section will guide you through the pre-approval process, the documents required, and how to compare different mortgage offers to find the best deal.

Understanding Pre-approval

Pre-approval is a process where a lender evaluates your financial background-your income, debt, credit history, and savings-to determine how much they are willing to lend you and at what interest rate. Unlike pre-qualification, which is a quick assessment, pre- approval involves a more thorough review, including a credit check and financial documentation.

Why Pre-approval Matters

Competitive Edge: In a seller's market, being pre-approved can set you apart from other buyers, showing sellers that your offer is serious and backed by lender support.

Budgeting Accuracy: Knowing exactly how much you can borrow helps refine your home search to properties within your budget, saving time and effort.

Faster Closing: Having pre-approval can speed up the closing process since much of your financial vetting is already completed.

The Pre-approval Process

Research Lenders: Start by researching potential lenders, including banks, credit unions, and online lenders, to compare rates and fees.

Submit an Application: You'll need to fill out a mortgage application with your chosen lender. This may involve a fee.

Provide Necessary Documentation: Lenders typically require documentation to verify your income, assets, debt, and credit history. Common documents include:

- Tax returns and W-2s or 1099s from the past two years.
- Pay stubs or other proof of current employment and income.
- Statements from all bank and investment accounts.
- Identification, such as a driver's license or passport.

Credit Check: The lender will perform a hard credit inquiry to assess your creditworthiness.

Receive Your Pre-approval Letter: If approved, the lender will issue a pre-approval letter stating how much you can borrow. Note that pre-approval letters are typically valid for 60 to 90 days.

Tips for a Successful Pre-approval

Improve Your Credit Score: Before applying, take steps to improve your credit score, as a higher score can qualify you for better loan terms.

Reduce Debt: Lowering your debt-to-income ratio by paying down debt can increase the amount you're eligible to borrow.

Stay Consistent in Your Employment: Lenders look for stable income when approving loans, so avoid changing jobs if possible during the pre-approval and home buying process.

Avoid New Credit Activities: Don't open new credit accounts or make significant purchases on credit before or during the pre-approval process, as this can affect your credit score and debt-to-income ratio.

Chapter 3
Finding The Right Home

Working with a Real Estate Agent

Selecting a knowledgeable and experienced real estate agent can make a significant difference in your home search. This section will outline the benefits of working with an agent, such as access to listings that may not be publicly available, negotiation expertise, and guidance through the closing process. Tips on finding the right agent, including interviewing potential candidates and checking references, will be provided to ensure a good fit for your home buying journey.

The Role of a Real Estate Agent

Real estate agents are licensed professionals who act as intermediaries between buyers and sellers in real estate transactions. For buyers, agents can:
- Provide access to listings and market information not easily available to the public.
- Arrange showings and help evaluate properties.
- Offer insights into neighborhoods, schools, and market trends.
- Assist in negotiating purchase terms and price.
- Guide you through the closing process, ensuring all necessary paperwork and legal requirements are met.

Finding the Right Agent

Selecting an agent who understands your needs and preferences is crucial. Here's how to find a good match:

Ask for Referrals: Friends, family, and colleagues who have recently bought homes can provide recommendations.

Research Online: Look for agents with good reviews and a strong presence in your target area.

Interview Prospects: Meet with several agents to discuss your needs and assess their experience, knowledge, and compatibility with your communication style.

Check Credentials: Ensure the agent is licensed and inquire about any additional certifications that might be relevant to your search.

Making the Most of Your Agent Relationship

To ensure a productive partnership, consider the following tips:

Communicate Clearly: Be upfront about your needs, budget, and deal-breakers. Regular, open communication helps your agent better serve you.

Understand the Agent's Role: Knowing what your agent can and cannot do for you demystifies the process and sets realistic expectations.

Be Open to Advice: Experienced agents offer valuable insights. While the final decisions are yours, consider their advice, especially on market trends and offer strategies.

Respect Their Time: While agents are there to help you, they often juggle multiple clients. Scheduling and feedback are important for maintaining a good working relationship.

The Buyer-Agent Agreement

When you decide to work with an agent, you may be asked to sign a buyer-agent agreement. This contract outlines the agent's duties to you, the duration of the agreement, and compensation (usually paid by the seller). Understand the terms before signing and discuss any concerns with your agent.

Benefits of Working with an Agent

Market Knowledge: Agents have in-depth knowledge of the market conditions, which can help you make informed decisions.

Negotiation Skills: They can negotiate on your behalf, potentially saving you money and avoiding pitfalls.

Professional Network: Agents have access to a network of professionals (e.g., inspectors, lawyers, contractors) who can assist during and after the purchase process.

Emotional Support: Buying a home can be stressful. A good agent can provide emotional support and guidance through challenging decisions.

Evaluating Homes Based on Your 'Must-Have' List

Having a clear 'must-have' list is crucial when evaluating potential homes. This section will guide you on how to stay focused on their priorities without getting sidetracked by less important features. It will also cover the importance of visualizing your life in the space and considering any necessary renovations or changes.

Creating a Comprehensive 'Must-Have' List

Your 'must-have' list should reflect your lifestyle, needs, and long-term goals. Consider including:

- Size Requirements: Number of bedrooms and bathrooms, square footage, and layout.
- Location Preferences: Proximity to work, schools, amenities, and community aspects.
- Essential Features: Specifics like a garage, a large kitchen, outdoor space, or accessibility features.
- Non-Negotiables: Anything you absolutely cannot compromise on, such as being in a particular school district or having a home office.

Using Your List to Screen Properties

With your list in hand, you can start screening properties effectively:

Online Listings: Use online real estate platforms to filter properties that match your basic criteria, such as location, price, and size.

Agent Collaboration: Share your list with your real estate agent. Their experience and network can help identify properties that fit your needs, some of which may not be publicly listed yet.

Prioritize Your List: Understand that finding a home that ticks every single box might be challenging. Prioritize your list into 'must-haves' and 'nice-to-haves'.

Assessing Homes During Showings

When visiting homes, use your list to assess each property critically:

Bring a Copy: Have your list with you during showings to check off items as you go through the house.

Take Notes and Photos: Document features that meet your criteria and those that don't. Photos can help recall details after you've seen multiple properties.

Assess Potential: Sometimes, a home might not meet all your criteria but has the potential to. Consider the cost and feasibility of making changes.

Evaluating the Compromise

In a competitive market or with a tight budget, you might need to compromise on some items:
Deal Breakers vs. Preferences: Distinguish between what you absolutely need and what you can live without or change over time.
Cost of Changes: Evaluate the cost of potential renovations or additions. Can you afford to make a property your perfect home after purchase?
Long-Term Satisfaction: Consider whether the compromises will affect your long-term satisfaction with the home.

Making Informed Decisions

Armed with your 'must-have' list and a thorough evaluation of each property, you can make informed decisions about which homes to pursue further. Remember, the goal is to find a home that meets your most important needs and feels right for you and your family.

By diligently applying your 'must-have' list during the home search and evaluation process, you ensure that the properties you consider seriously are those that truly align with your essential requirements. This strategic approach saves time, reduces stress, and increases the likelihood of finding a home that you'll be happy with in the long run.

The Importance of Home Inspections and Appraisals

Home inspections and appraisals are critical steps in the home buying process, providing peace of mind and protecting your investment. This section will explain the purpose of a home inspection, what it entails, and how it can affect the negotiation process. It will also cover the role of appraisals in determining the home's value for mortgage purposes and how both can impact your decision to proceed with the purchase.

Home Inspections: Ensuring Safety and Identifying Repairs

A home inspection is a thorough examination of the physical structure and systems of a home, from the roof to the foundation. Here's why it's essential:

- Identify Safety Issues: Inspectors look for safety concerns, such as electrical problems, poor insulation, and structural issues, that could pose risks to occupants.
- Reveal Illegal Additions or Installations: The inspection can uncover modifications made without proper permits, which could affect the property's insurance, usability, and value.
- Estimate Future Costs: Inspectors can provide an estimate of the lifespan of major systems

(like heating and cooling) and components (such as the roof and windows), helping buyers plan for future expenses.
- Negotiation Leverage: Significant issues revealed by an inspection can be used to negotiate repairs or adjust the purchase price.

The Home Inspection Process

Choosing an Inspector: Look for a licensed, experienced professional. Consider recommendations from your real estate agent or reviews from previous clients.

Attending the Inspection: Buyers are usually encouraged to attend the inspection. It's an opportunity to ask questions and learn about the condition of the home.

Reviewing the Report: After the inspection, you'll receive a report detailing the findings. Review it carefully and discuss any concerns with your agent.

Appraisals: Valuing the Property

An appraisal is an unbiased professional opinion of a home's value, typically required by lenders to ensure the property is worth the loan amount.

Lender Requirement: Most mortgage lenders require an appraisal to protect their investment, ensuring the loan doesn't exceed the home's value.

Determining Property Value: Appraisers consider recent sales of similar properties, the home's condition, location, and any unique features to determine its value.

Influence on Loan Amount: If an appraisal comes in lower than the offer price, buyers may need to renegotiate the price with the seller, make up the difference, or withdraw their offer.

Why Appraisals Matter

Protection for Buyers: An appraisal can prevent you from overpaying for a home. It provides a safety net, ensuring you pay a fair price based on current market conditions.

Impact on Financing: The appraisal affects the amount a lender is willing to provide. A low appraisal may require renegotiating the deal or finding additional funds.

Navigating Inspection and Appraisal Challenges

Inspection Contingencies: Offers can include an inspection contingency, allowing buyers to back out or renegotiate based on the inspection results.

Appraisal Contingencies: Similarly, an appraisal contingency can protect buyers if the appraisal comes in low, offering an opportunity to renegotiate or cancel the contract without penalty.

Understanding the roles of home inspections and appraisals in the home buying process emphasizes their importance in making informed decisions and securing a sound investment. Both provide critical information that can affect the viability of a home purchase, influence negotiations, and impact the overall financial commitment to a property.

Chapter 4
Making An Offer And Negotiating

Understanding the Current Market

The real estate market fluctuates between being a buyer's market, where the advantage is with the buyer due to a surplus of homes, and a seller's market, characterized by a shortage of inventory giving sellers the upper hand. This section will explain how to assess the current market conditions and adjust your offer and negotiation strategies accordingly.

Seller's Market

In a seller's market, demand exceeds supply. There are more buyers looking for homes than there are homes available. This scenario typically results in:

- Higher Prices: Competition among buyers can drive up home prices.
- Faster Sales: Homes tend to sell quickly, sometimes within days of listing.
- Multiple Offers: Sellers may receive multiple offers, often above the asking price.
- Strategy for Buyers: In a seller's market, it's crucial to act quickly, make competitive offers, and be prepared to negotiate less and accommodate seller preferences.

Buyer's Market

Conversely, a buyer's market is characterized by a surplus of homes for sale compared to the number of buyers. This situation usually leads to:

- Lower Prices: Buyers have more leverage to negotiate lower prices.

- More Choices: A larger inventory of homes means more options for buyers.
- Longer Sales Times: Homes may stay on the market longer, creating opportunities for buyers to negotiate more favorable terms.
- Strategy for Buyers: Buyers can afford to be choosier and negotiate harder on price and terms. It's also an opportunity to ask for extras, like closing costs or repairs.

Balanced Market

- A balanced market occurs when supply and demand are about equal. Neither buyers nor sellers have a distinct advantage, leading to:
- Stable Prices: Home prices tend to increase at a steady, predictable rate.
- Reasonable Offers: Sellers are open to negotiation but won't face the pressure to accept lowball offers.
- Strategy for Buyers: Buyers should focus on making fair offers based on comparable sales and market conditions. There's room for negotiation, but excessive lowballing can lead to missed opportunities.

Assessing the Market

Understanding which market you're entering as a buyer involves:

- Research: Follow local real estate listings, noting how long homes stay on the market and whether they sell for asking price.
- Professional Insight: Work with a real estate agent knowledgeable about local market conditions. They can provide valuable advice on crafting your buying strategy.
- Flexibility: Be prepared to adjust your strategy as market conditions change. Flexibility can make the difference in successfully purchasing a home.

The Impact of Market Conditions

Market conditions can significantly impact your buying experience:

- Timing: In a seller's market, you may need to act quickly and decisively. In a buyer's market, you might have more time to decide.
- Negotiation: Your ability to negotiate terms and extras varies greatly with market conditions.
- Expectations: Align your expectations with the current market. In a seller's market, expect competition; in a buyer's market, look for opportunities to get more for your money.

By understanding the current real estate market, buyers can tailor their approach to finding and purchasing a home, maximizing their chances of success regardless of market conditions. This knowledge is crucial for setting realistic expectations and developing effective strategies for navigating the home buying process.

Understanding the Current Market

The real estate market fluctuates between being a buyer's market, where the advantage is with the buyer due to a surplus of homes, and a seller's market, characterized by a shortage of inventory giving sellers the upper hand. This section will explain how to assess the current market conditions and adjust your offer and negotiation strategies accordingly.

Analyzing Market Trends

To navigate the real estate market effectively, it's crucial to understand underlying trends:

- Historical Data: Look at price trends, inventory levels, and days on market over the past few years to identify patterns.
- Interest Rates: Monitor changes in mortgage interest rates, as they can influence buyer demand and affordability.
- Economic Indicators: Employment rates, economic growth, and consumer confidence can affect real estate market conditions.

Adapting to Market Fluctuations

Flexibility and adaptability are key in responding to market conditions:

Seller's Market Strategies:

- **Pre-approval**: Have your mortgage pre-approval in hand to make your offer more attractive.
- **Flexibility on Terms**: Consider being flexible with closing dates or waiving certain contingencies to make your offer stand out.
- **Act Fast**: Be prepared to make quick decisions without compromising on your essential criteria.

Buyer's Market Strategies:

- **Negotiate Aggressively**: Use the surplus of inventory to negotiate on price, closing costs, or repairs.
- **Wider Search**: Expand your search criteria to consider homes that might need a bit of work or are in less competitive areas.
- **Patience**: Take your time to find the right home at the right price, knowing you have less competition.

Leveraging Technology

Utilize online tools and platforms to stay informed and make educated decisions:

- **Real Estate Websites**: Use these for comprehensive market analysis, including virtual tours and neighborhood statistics.
- **Mobile Apps**: Apps can provide instant notifications on new listings or price changes in your desired area.
- **Social Media and Forums**: Local real estate groups can offer insider insights and firsthand experiences from current homebuyers.

Working with Market Experts

Engage professionals who understand the nuances of the market:

- **Real Estate Agents**: A knowledgeable agent can provide advice tailored to current conditions and help you navigate the buying process.
- **Financial Advisors**: They can offer guidance on budgeting and financing strategies that align with market conditions and your personal financial goals.
- **Local Insiders**: Contractors, home inspectors, and local residents can offer valuable insights into specific neighborhoods and properties.

Leveraging Technology

Utilize online tools and platforms to stay informed and make educated decisions:

- **Real Estate Websites**: Use these for comprehensive market analysis, including virtual tours and neighborhood statistics.
- **Mobile Apps**: Apps can provide instant notifications on new listings or price changes in your desired area.
- **Social Media and Forums**: Local real estate groups can offer insider insights and firsthand experiences from current homebuyers.

Working with Market Experts

Engage professionals who understand the nuances of the market:

- **Real Estate Agents**: A knowledgeable agent can provide advice tailored to current conditions and help you navigate the buying process.
- **Financial Advisors**: They can offer guidance on budgeting and financing strategies that align with market conditions and your personal financial goals.

- **Local Insiders**: Contractors, home inspectors, and local residents can offer valuable insights into specific neighborhoods and properties.

Staying Informed and Proactive

Keeping abreast of market changes is crucial:

- **Regular Updates**: Subscribe to real estate newsletters and market analysis reports.
- **Educational Resources**: Attend webinars, workshops, and seminars on real estate trends and buying strategies.
- **Network**: Connect with other buyers, sellers, and industry professionals to exchange information and strategies.

Understanding the current market deeply and adjusting your strategy accordingly can significantly enhance your home buying experience. By staying informed, flexible, and proactive, you can navigate the complexities of the market more effectively, making smarter decisions that align with your homeownership goals. Whether facing a seller's or buyer's market, your ability to adapt will be a considerable advantage.

Negotiating with Sellers

Negotiation is an art that can lead to significant savings and better terms in your home purchase. This section will offer strategies for effective negotiation, such as understanding the seller's motivations, when to compromise, and how to communicate through your real estate agent. It will also touch on common negotiation points beyond price, including repairs, closing costs, and move-in dates.

Research and Preparation

- **Understand the Market**: Knowing whether you're in a buyer's or seller's market can guide your negotiation strategy. In a seller's market, you may have less room to negotiate, while a buyer's market might offer more leverage.
- **Analyze the Property's Time on Market**: Homes that have been listed for a long time may

have sellers who are more willing to negotiate.
- **Review Comparable Sales**: Look at recent sales of similar homes in the area to determine a fair offer price.

Making the Initial Offer

- Start with a Fair Offer: An offer that's too low can offend sellers and close the door on negotiation. Your opening offer should be competitive yet leave room for negotiation.
- Highlight Your Strengths as a Buyer: A pre-approval letter, flexibility on closing dates, or fewer contingencies can make your offer more attractive.

During the Negotiation

- Focus on Win-Win Solutions: Try to understand the seller's priorities, such as a longer or shorter closing period, and see if you can accommodate them in exchange for a better price or terms.
- Use Inspection Results: If the home inspection reveals issues, use it as a negotiation point to lower the price or ask the seller to make repairs.
- Be Prepared to Compromise: Identify areas where you're willing to give in and those where you're not. This flexibility can help close the deal.

Communication and Tactics

- Use Your Agent: Let your real estate agent lead the negotiation. They have the experience and detachment to negotiate effectively on your behalf.
- Stay Calm and Patient: Negotiations can take time, and showing desperation or frustration can weaken your position.
- Be Ready to Walk Away: If the deal doesn't meet your minimum requirements or feels wrong, be prepared to walk away. This position can sometimes bring the seller back to the table with a better offer.

After an Agreement Is Reached

Get Everything in Writing: Once you reach a verbal agreement, ensure all terms are detailed in a written contract. This includes the agreed-upon price, any concessions, closing date, and contingencies.

Review the Contract Carefully: Ensure all negotiated terms are accurately reflected before signing. This is also a good time to review any contingencies to ensure you're protected.

Effective negotiation is a blend of art and science, requiring research, strategy, and interpersonal skills. By understanding the seller's position and leveraging your own strengths, you can navigate the negotiation process to achieve a favorable outcome. Whether it's adjusting the offer based on home inspection results, finding common ground on closing dates, or knowing when to walk away, successful negotiation can significantly impact the home buying process.

Contingencies to Consider

Including contingencies in your offer can provide protection against unforeseen issues, but they must be used wisely to avoid weakening your proposal. This section will explain key contingencies, such as home inspections, financing, and appraisal, detailing how they work and when to include them in your offer.

Inspection Contingency

This contingency allows the buyer to have the property inspected within a specified period. It's crucial because:

- It reveals the home's true condition, including potential costly repairs or safety issues that aren't obvious during a showing.
- Gives leverage to negotiate repairs or credit with the seller before finalizing the purchase.
- Option to withdraw if significant issues are discovered and an agreement can't be reached with the seller.

Financing Contingency

Also known as a mortgage contingency, it ensures that:

- The deal is contingent on the buyer securing financing from a bank or mortgage lender. If the buyer's financing falls through, they can exit the contract penalty-free.
- Protects the buyer from losing their earnest money deposit if they can't finalize a loan.
- Time-sensitive, usually requiring buyers to obtain a loan within a certain period.

Appraisal Contingency

This contingency is tied to the property's appraisal value:

- Ensures the home is valued at a minimum specified amount, which is typically the sale price or higher.
- Protects the buyer from overpaying for the property. If the appraisal comes in lower than the agreed price, the buyer can renegotiate or opt out.
- Critical for securing financing, as lenders often base the loan amount on the appraised value.

Title Contingency

Ensures the property title is clear of issues, meaning:

- The seller has the legal right to sell the property, and there are no liens or disputes over property ownership.
- Allows for a thorough review of the title history to ensure no encumbrances or problems could affect ownership.
- Buyers can back out or negotiate solutions if title issues are discovered.

Home Sale Contingency

For buyers who need to sell their current home to finance a new one, this contingency:

- Makes the new home purchase contingent on the sale of the buyer's current home.
- Provides a safety net for buyers who can't afford two mortgages simultaneously.
- Can make offers less attractive to sellers in competitive markets due to the uncertainty it introduces.

How to Use Contingencies Effectively

- Understand Your Needs: Tailor contingencies to your specific situation. Not all contingencies may be necessary, and some can make your offer less competitive.
- Negotiate Wisely: Use contingencies as leverage in negotiations. For instance, you might waive certain contingencies in a competitive market to strengthen your offer but insist on others for protection.
- Timelines Matter: Be mindful of the timelines associated with each contingency. Prompt action and decision-making are crucial to keeping the transaction moving smoothly.

Leveraging contingencies wisely can protect buyers from various risks involved in purchasing a home, from hidden defects and financing falls through to overpaying based on an inaccurate appraisal. While strategically using contingencies, it's also essential to balance their protective benefits with the competitiveness of your offer, especially in hot markets. Consulting with a real estate professional can help navigate these nuances effectively.

Chapter 5
Securing Financing

Choosing the Right Mortgage Type

There are various types of mortgages available, each with its own set of rules, interest rates, and payment terms. This section will provide an overview of the most common types of mortgages, including fixed-rate, adjustable-rate, FHA loans, VA loans, and more. It will guide readers on how to choose the best mortgage type based on their financial situation, future plans, and risk tolerance.

Understanding Mortgage Types

Fixed-Rate Mortgages (FRM)

Fixed-rate mortgages have the same interest rate for the entire repayment term, resulting in consistent monthly payments.
- Pros: Predictability in payments; protection from rising interest rates.
- Cons: Higher initial interest rates compared to adjustable-rate mortgages.
- Best For: Buyers planning to stay in their homes for a long time and those who prefer stable payments.

Adjustable-Rate Mortgages (ARM)

Adjustable-rate mortgages start with a fixed interest rate for a set period, after which the rate adjusts periodically based on market conditions.
- Pros: Lower initial interest rates, which can result in lower initial monthly payments.
- Cons: Future rate increases can significantly raise monthly payments.
- Best For: Buyers who plan to sell or refinance before the end of the initial fixed-rate period, or who expect their income to rise.

Government-Insured Mortgages

This category includes FHA loans, VA loans, and USDA loans, each designed to meet the needs of specific groups of homebuyers.

FHA Loans: Require lower minimum credit scores and down payments. Best for first-time buyers or those with lower credit scores.

VA Loans: Available to veterans and active military members, offering loans with no down payment. Best for eligible service members seeking low upfront costs.

USDA Loans: Designed for rural homebuyers, offering zero down payment loans in eligible areas. Best for buyers in rural areas who meet income requirements.

Choosing the Right Mortgage

When selecting a mortgage type, consider:

Financial Stability: Fixed-rate mortgages offer stability, while ARMs might be an option if you expect your financial situation to improve.
Homeownership Goals: If you plan to move or refinance in a few years, an ARM could offer lower initial payments.
Down Payment: Assess how much you can afford upfront. Government-insured loans can be beneficial for those with lower down payments.
Credit Score: Higher credit scores open the door to better terms and rates, particularly for conventional loans.

It's also wise to consult with a mortgage broker or lender who can provide insights based on your financial profile and the current market conditions. Preparing questions in advance can help ensure you cover all necessary grounds during your consultation.

Choosing the right mortgage is a crucial step in the home buying process, significantly affecting your financial future. By understanding the different types of mortgages and how they align with your financial situation and homeownership goals, you can make an informed decision that sets you up for long-term success.

Mortgage Application Process

Applying for a mortgage can be a daunting process, involving a lot of paperwork and strict qualifications. This section will walk you through the steps of the mortgage application process, from gathering the necessary documentation to understanding what lenders look for in applicants. Tips on how to streamline the process and improve the chances of approval will also be included.

Step 1: Pre-Approval

Purpose: Provides an estimate of how much you can borrow based on your financial information.

Process: You submit financial documents, including proof of income, assets, and credit history, to a lender. The lender assesses your creditworthiness and issues a pre- approval letter.

Benefit: Pre-approval helps you shop for homes within your budget and strengthens your position when making an offer.

Step 2: Finding a Home and Making an Offer

Action: Once pre-approved, you search for a home. Upon finding the right property, you make an offer and negotiate terms.

Context: Your pre-approval amount guides your budget. The offer may include contingencies that affect the mortgage process, such as an appraisal or inspection.

Step 3: Formal Mortgage Application

Trigger: Your offer on a home is accepted.

Process: You select a mortgage type and submit a formal application. This involves providing more detailed financial information and possibly paying an application fee.

Documents Required: Updated financial statements, tax returns, employment verification, and details about the property.

Step 4: Loan Processing

Overview: The lender verifies your financial information, checks your credit history, and assesses the property details.
Appraisal: An appraisal is ordered to determine the property's value.
Underwriting: The lender's underwriting team reviews all information to ensure compliance with loan requirements.

Step 5: Conditional Approval and Further Verification

Outcome: If the lender is satisfied, they issue a conditional approval, which may require further verification or documents.
Possible Requirements: Additional proof of income, clarification on credit history, or additional inspections.

Tips for a Smooth Mortgage Application Process

Stay Organized: Keep all your financial documents in order and readily accessible.
Be Responsive: Promptly respond to lender requests for information or documentation to avoid delays.
Maintain Financial Stability: Avoid making large purchases, taking on new debt, or changing jobs during the mortgage application process.
Review Documents Carefully: Understand all the terms of your mortgage and ask questions about anything unclear.

Understanding each step of the mortgage application process helps set realistic expectations and prepares you for the tasks and decisions ahead. By staying informed and proactive, you can navigate this process more confidently and secure a mortgage that fits your financial goals.

Home Insurance Requirements

Most lenders require borrowers to have home insurance as a condition of the mortgage. This section will explain why home insurance is necessary, what it covers, and how to choose the right policy. It will also discuss the process of escrowing insurance payments with your mortgage payment and how to compare insurance quotes to get the best rate and coverage.

Why You Need Home Insurance

Protection Against Losses: Home insurance covers damage from fires, storms, theft, and other unforeseen events, helping you to repair, rebuild, or replace your home and belongings.

Liability Coverage: It protects you in case someone is injured on your property, covering legal fees and medical bills.

Lender Requirements: Most mortgage lenders require you to have homeowner's insurance as a condition of the loan to protect their investment in your property.

Types of Coverage

- Dwelling Coverage: Pays to repair or rebuild your home if it's damaged by an insured event.
- Personal Property Coverage: Covers the cost of replacing your belongings if they are stolen or destroyed.
- Liability Protection: Covers legal costs for injury or property damage from accidents on your property.
- Additional Living Expenses (ALE): Pays for your living costs if you must temporarily relocate while your home is being repaired.

How Much Coverage Do You Need?

- Dwelling Coverage: Should be enough to rebuild your home at current construction costs. Consult with a construction professional or use online calculators to get an estimate.
- Personal Property: Typically set at 50-70% of dwelling coverage. Conducting a home

inventory can help you decide if you need additional coverage.
- Liability Coverage: The amount can vary, but homeowners should consider enough coverage to protect their assets in case of a lawsuit.

Choosing a Policy

- Compare Quotes: Get quotes from multiple insurance companies to compare coverage options and prices.
- Understand Policy Limits and Deductibles: Know the maximum amount the policy will pay out and how much you need to pay out-of-pocket before coverage kicks in.
- Consider Special Coverage: If you live in areas prone to floods or earthquakes, you may need additional policies, as standard home insurance doesn't cover these disasters.

The Role of the Home Appraisal

Determining Replacement Cost: The home appraisal can help in determining the dwelling coverage amount by providing an estimate of the home's value and replacement cost.

Maintaining Your Policy

- Review Annually: Your insurance needs can change. Review your policy yearly to ensure it meets your current needs.
- Update Coverage for Renovations: If you make significant improvements to your home, update your policy to reflect the increased value.

Home insurance is a crucial part of homeownership, offering financial protection against a wide range of risks. Understanding the requirements, coverage options, and how to choose the right policy ensures that your investment is well protected. While navigating the home buying process, take the time to thoroughly research and select a home insurance policy that meets your specific needs, providing peace of mind as you embark on the journey of homeownership.

Chapter 6
Closing The Deal

The Closing Process and Finalizing Your Mortgage

Closing on a home is the final step in the home buying process, where the property's ownership is officially transferred from the seller to the buyer. This section will detail what to expect during the closing process, including closing costs, the documents you will need to sign, and how to prepare for your closing day. It will also cover the final steps in finalizing your mortgage, including the final approval and funding of your loan.

The Closing Process Explained

Closing, also known as settlement, is when the purchase of the home is finalized, and ownership is officially transferred from the seller to the buyer. This section will outline the typical steps of the closing process, including a review of the closing disclosure, the final walkthrough of the property, and the signing of various legal and financial documents. It will also explain the roles of the individuals involved in the closing process, such as the closing agent, attorneys, and real estate agents.

Preparing for Closing

- Final Walkthrough: Conducted 24 hours before closing, this is the buyer's last chance to verify the property's condition and ensure agreed-upon repairs have been made.
- Review Closing Disclosure: Lenders must provide a Closing Disclosure at least three days before closing. This document details the final loan terms, closing costs, and any outstanding

fees. Compare it with the initial Loan Estimate to ensure accuracy.

Key Participants

- Closing Agent: A neutral third party, often a title company or attorney, who oversees the closing process, ensuring all documents are executed and recorded correctly.
- Buyers and Sellers: Both parties sign various documents, though they might not always be present together.
- Real Estate Agents: Agents may attend to provide support and clarify any questions.
- Lender's Representative: Sometimes present to address any last-minute loan details.

Important Documents

- Mortgage Note: Legally binds you to the loan terms, including the obligation to repay.
- Deed: Transfers ownership from the seller to the buyer.
- Closing Disclosure: Summarizes the final financial terms of the mortgage.
- Bill of Sale: Lists any personal property (like appliances or furniture) included in the home purchase.
- Title and Title Insurance: Ensures the buyer is receiving a clear title. Title insurance protects against future claims against the property.

Closing Costs

What Are They? Expenses over and above the property price, including loan origination fees, appraisal fees, title searches, title insurance, taxes, and other prepaid items like homeowner's insurance.

Who Pays What? Closing costs are typically 2-5% of the home's purchase price. The buyer usually bears most of the cost, but some fees can be negotiated with the seller.

The Day of Closing

- Signing Documents: Expect to sign a lot of paperwork. The closing agent will guide you through each document, explaining its purpose.
- Transferring Funds: Buyers must bring the required amount for closing costs and the down payment, often in the form of a cashier's check or wire transfer.
- Receiving the Keys: Once all documents are signed and funds distributed, you officially become the homeowner and receive the keys to your new home.

Post-Closing Responsibilities

- Record the Deed: The closing agent usually handles this, filing the deed with the county to

make the transfer of ownership public record.
- Settle into Your New Home: Begin the move-in process, but also keep all closing documents in a safe place for future reference, especially for tax purposes or future refinancing

The closing process is the final hurdle in the home buying journey. While it can be complex and time-consuming, understanding each step can significantly ease the transition from buyer to homeowner. Being well-prepared, asking questions, and ensuring you have all necessary documents and funds ready can help make closing day a smooth and enjoyable experience.

Post-Closing Considerations

Once the closing is complete, and you have the keys to your new home, there are several immediate actions you should take. This section will cover important post-closing tasks such as filing your deed with the county, setting up utilities, changing your address, and securing the property. It will also discuss the importance of maintaining a good relationship with your lender and understanding your mortgage servicing rights.

Securing Your Home

- Change the Locks: You can't be sure who has copies of the keys from the previous owner, so changing locks is a priority for safety.
- Install a Security System: If the home doesn't already have one, consider installing a security system for added protection.
- Safety Check: Test smoke detectors, carbon monoxide detectors, and fire extinguishers. Replace batteries and ensure they're in working order.

Managing Your Mortgage and Finances

- First Mortgage Payment: Know when your first mortgage payment is due and consider setting up automatic payments to never miss a deadline.
- Escrow Account Review: If your property taxes and homeowner's insurance are paid through an escrow account with your mortgage, review the account statements to ensure payments

are made on time.
- Budget for Home Maintenance: Start setting aside money for regular maintenance and unexpected repairs. A good rule of thumb is to save 1-3% of your home's purchase price annually for maintenance.

Updating Your Address

- Postal Service: Change your address with the postal service to ensure you receive mail at your new home.
- Update Important Documents: Notify banks, employers, and other important institutions of your new address. Don't forget to update your driver's license and vehicle registration if required by your state.

Utilities and Services

- Transfer Utilities: Make sure utilities like water, electricity, gas, and internet are transferred to your name and are operational.
- Maintenance Contracts: If the previous owner had any maintenance contracts or warranties (for appliances, HVAC system, etc.), make sure they are transferred to you or start new ones if necessary.

Getting to Know Your New Community

- Meet the Neighbors: Introduce yourself to your neighbors. They can be a valuable resource for local information and services.
- Explore Local Amenities: Find out where essential services are located, such as hospitals, pharmacies, grocery stores, and schools.
- Community Involvement: Look into local community groups or social media pages to stay informed about neighborhood events and news.

Home Improvements and Personalization

- Prioritize Projects: Make a list of desired home improvements, prioritizing those that need immediate attention.
- Decorating: Start personalizing your space to reflect your style and make your house feel like home.

Important Documents and Records

Organize Important Papers: Keep all documents related to the home purchase, closing, home warranty, and insurance policies in a safe, easily accessible place.

Maintenance Records: Maintain a file for receipts and warranties for any home improvements or repairs. This can be valuable for future selling points or warranty claims.

Navigating the post-closing period with these considerations in mind can help new homeowners settle in more comfortably and securely. It's a time of transition that requires attention to detail but also offers the excitement of making a new house your home. With careful planning and organization, you can enjoy the beginnings of homeownership while laying the groundwork for a stable and rewarding future in your new residence.

Planning for Homeownership Responsibilities

The transition from homebuyer to homeowner brings a new set of responsibilities. This section will touch on the essentials of homeownership, including regular maintenance tasks, understanding property taxes and insurance, and planning for future home improvements. It will offer advice on budgeting for unexpected repairs and the importance of building a network of trusted professionals for maintenance and repair work.

Regular Maintenance and Repairs

Seasonal Maintenance: Create a seasonal maintenance checklist to ensure tasks like gutter cleaning, HVAC system servicing, and roof inspections are done timely to prevent larger issues.

Preventative Maintenance: Regularly check for and address minor problems, such as leaks, cracks, or peeling paint, to avoid costly repairs in the future.

Emergency Repairs: Set aside a fund for unexpected repairs. Knowing local service providers for plumbing, electrical, or HVAC emergencies is also crucial.

Financial Management

Mortgage Payments: Stay on top of monthly mortgage payments to avoid penalties or, in extreme cases, foreclosure. Consider setting up automatic payments for convenience.
Property Taxes and Insurance: Understand when property taxes are due and ensure your homeowner's insurance is up-to-date, adjusting coverage as needed for home improvements or changes in property value.
Utility Bills: Budget for regular utility bills, including water, electricity, gas, and internet. Look into energy-efficient improvements to help manage costs.

Safety and Security

Home Security System: Consider investing in a home security system to protect your property and family. Even basic measures like outdoor lighting can enhance security.

Fire Safety: Install smoke detectors on every floor and in sleeping areas. Regularly check that they work and replace batteries as needed. Have fire extinguishers accessible in key areas, especially the kitchen.

Carbon Monoxide Detectors: Ensure your home is equipped with carbon monoxide detectors, particularly if you have gas appliances or an attached garage.

Energy Efficiency

Energy Audits: Conduct or hire a professional for an energy audit to identify ways to improve your home's energy efficiency, which can reduce utility bills and increase comfort.

Upgrades and Improvements: Consider energy-efficient upgrades, such as LED lighting, high-efficiency appliances, and proper insulation, to reduce energy consumption.

Lawn Care and Landscaping

Regular Maintenance: Keep your lawn and garden well-maintained to enhance curb appeal and use. This includes mowing, weeding, and pruning.

Landscaping Projects: Plan landscaping projects that can improve your property's value and your enjoyment of the space, considering both aesthetics and functionality.

Being a Good Neighbor

Community Engagement: Participate in neighborhood events and organizations to build relationships and contribute to your community's well-being.

Property Boundaries: Respect property lines and shared spaces. Communicate openly with neighbors about any issues or projects that may affect them.

Long-Term Planning

Home Improvements: Plan and budget for long-term home improvement projects that can enhance your lifestyle and increase your home's value.

Resale Considerations: Keep potential resale in mind when making significant changes or improvements, focusing on updates that will appeal to future buyers.

Embracing these homeownership responsibilities ensures that your home remains a safe, comfortable, and valuable asset. While the list may seem daunting, taking it step by step and planning for regular upkeep can make these tasks manageable and even rewarding. Remember, maintaining and improving your home not only benefits you today but also contributes to its long-term value and appeal.

Chapter 7
Moving In

Initial Planning

Create a Moving Timeline: Establish a timeline leading up to moving day, including key tasks like hiring movers, packing, and setting up utilities in your new home.

Budget for Moving Expenses: Outline all potential expenses, including moving company fees, packing supplies, and any new furniture or household items you'll need. Don't forget to account for unexpected costs.

Hiring Professional Movers vs. DIV Move

Professional Movers: For a less stressful experience, consider hiring professional movers. Obtain quotes from several reputable companies, check reviews, and ensure they are licensed and insured.

DIV Move: If you're considering moving yourself, assess the volume of your belongings, the distance of your move, and whether you can enlist the help of friends or family. Renting a moving truck and purchasing packing supplies will be key tasks.

Packing Strategies

Declutter Before Packing: Sort through your belongings and decide what to keep, sell, donate, or throw away. This reduces the amount of stuff you need to move and helps start fresh in your new home.
Start Early: Begin packing non-essential items weeks in advance. Label boxes with their contents and intended room in the new house.
Essentials Box: Pack a box of essentials you'll need immediately upon arriving at your new home, including toiletries, medications, basic tools, and a few days' worth of clothing.

Managing Utilities and Services

Transfer or Cancel Services: Arrange to transfer services like internet and utilities to your new home or cancel them if you're moving out of the area. Do this well in advance to ensure you're not without essential services when you move in.

Change Your Address: Update your address with the postal service, banks, employers, and any subscription services to ensure you receive mail and packages at your new home.

Moving Day Logistics

Plan the Day: If hiring movers, confirm the time they'll arrive and the estimated duration of the move. If moving yourself, create a schedule for the day to keep everything on track.

Child and Pet Arrangements: Moving day can be chaotic, so consider arranging care for children and pets to keep them safe and reduce stress.

Settling In

Unpacking Plan: Prioritize unpacking essential rooms first, such as the kitchen and bedrooms. Gradually unpack other areas according to your needs and timeline.
Familiarize Yourself with the Neighborhood: Take walks, visit local businesses, and introduce yourself to neighbors to start feeling at home in your new community.

Emotional Considerations

Acknowledge the Transition: Moving can be emotionally challenging. Allow yourself and your family time to say goodbye to your old home and gradually acclimate to your new surroundings.

Stay Connected: Keep in touch with friends and family members from your previous location while also making an effort to meet new people in your new community.

Getting Involved in Your New Community

Moving to a new area means more than just a new house-it's about becoming part of a community. This section will suggest ways to get involved and meet neighbors, such as attending local events, joining community groups or clubs, and participating in neighborhood associations. It will highlight the benefits of community engagement, including making friends, networking opportunities, and enhancing your sense of belonging.

Meeting Neighbors

Introduce Yourself: Take the initiative to introduce yourself to your neighbors. A friendly greeting or a small gift, like baked goods, can break the ice.
Attend Neighborhood Gatherings: Block parties, homeowner association meetings, and local events are great places to meet people and learn about your community.
Utilize Community Spaces: Parks, community centers, and local businesses are natural gathering spots where you can meet neighbors and make new friends.

Volunteering

Find Local Organizations: Look for community centers, non-profits, schools, or environmental groups where you can volunteer. It's a rewarding way to meet people who share your interests.

Participate in Community Projects: Community gardens, clean-up days, and other local initiatives offer chances to contribute positively while interacting with residents.

Joining Clubs and Groups

Explore Your Interests: Join clubs or groups that align with your hobbies or interests. Whether it's a book club, sports league, gardening group, or a class at a local community college, these are excellent ways to connect.

Use Social Media and Apps: Platforms like Meetup or local Facebook groups can help you find gatherings or clubs in your area.

Engaging in Local Governance

Attend Town Meetings: Stay informed and involved in local issues by attending town or city council meetings. This can also be a platform for voicing concerns and contributing ideas.

Join a Local Board or Committee: If you're passionate about certain community aspects, consider joining a board or committee that focuses on those areas.

Supporting Local Businesses

Shop Locally: Regular visits to local shops, cafes, and markets not only support the local economy but also help you get to know the proprietors and fellow customers.

Attend Local Events: Farmer's markets, art shows, and festivals are not only fun but also great opportunities to meet people and learn about the cultural fabric of your community.

Staying Open and Positive

Be Open to New Experiences: Embrace the unique aspects of your new community. Trying new activities or attending different events can broaden your horizons and introduce you to new friends.

Maintain a Positive Outlook: Moving and adapting to a new community can have its challenges. Keeping a positive attitude and being open to building new relationships are key to a successful transition.

Conclusion

Congratulations on your new home! As this guide concludes, remember that homeownership is a journey filled with learning, growth, and occasional challenges. This chapter wraps up with encouragement for the new homeowner, emphasizing the importance of patience, continuous learning, and enjoying the process of making your house a home.

The journey of purchasing a home and transitioning into a new community is one of life's most significant milestones. It's a path filled with anticipation, challenges, and learning opportunities. From understanding the intricacies of the home buying process, securing financing, and navigating the complexities of moving, to the joy of making your new house a home and becoming an active member of your community, each step offers a chance to grow and create lasting memories.

Reflections on the Home Buying Process

The home buying process is as much about discovery as it is about acquisition. It teaches patience, diligence, and the importance of being informed and prepared. As you reflect on the journey, remember the moments of excitement at finding "the one," the negotiations that tested your resolve, and the satisfaction of finally holding the keys to your new home. These experiences, both challenging and rewarding, have led you to this point.

The Significance of Creating a Home

A house becomes a home not just through its walls and windows, but through the life and love you bring into it. Decorating and renovating allow you to imprint your personality and style, making your space truly yours. But it's the memories created within these walls-the quiet evenings, the gatherings of friends and family, and the personal milestones-that truly transform a house into a cherished home.

Becoming Part of a New Community

Integrating into a new community is an adventure in its own right. It offers the opportunity to meet new people, engage in local traditions, and contribute to the neighborhood's vibrancy. Embracing this new chapter opens up a world of possibilities for friendships, hobbies, and involvement that enriches your life beyond the confines of your home.

Looking Ahead

As you settle into your new home and community, remember that homeownership is an ongoing journey. There will be more to learn, challenges to face, and joys to celebrate. Continue to invest in your home, nurture relationships with neighbors, and engage with your community. These efforts will not only enhance your quality of life but also strengthen the bonds that transform a neighborhood into a community.

Final Thoughts

Congratulations on navigating the path to homeownership and taking the first steps into your new life in your new home and community. May your home be a haven of happiness, a place where memories are made, and a foundation for your future. Remember, the journey of homeownership is not just about the destination but about embracing each moment along the way.

Glossary

Adjustable-Rate Mortgage **(ARM):**
A type of mortgage loan where the interest rate adjusts over time based on market conditions, starting with an initial fixed rate.

Appraisal:
An evaluation to determine the property's value conducted by a professional appraiser, typically required by lenders to ensure the loan does not exceed the home's value.

Closing:
The final step in the home buying process where the title is transferred from the seller to the buyer, and the transaction is completed.

Closing Costs:
Expenses over and above the price of the property in a real estate transaction, including taxes, legal fees, and lender charges.

Contingency:
A condition outlined in a real estate contract that must be met for the transaction to proceed. Common contingencies include financing, inspection, and appraisal.

Deed:
A legal document that transfers ownership of property from one party to another.

Down Payment:
An initial payment made when buying a home, typically a percentage of the purchase price, with the remainder financed through a mortgage.

Equity:
The difference between the market value of a property and the amount still owed on its mortgage.

Fixed-Rate Mortgage (FRM):
A mortgage with a fixed interest rate for the entire term of the loan, resulting in consistent monthly payments.

Home Inspection:
An examination of a property's condition conducted by a qualified inspector, usually required by the buyer to identify any issues before completing the purchase.

Homeowner's Insurance:
Insurance coverage that protects homeowners against damage to their home and possessions, as well as liability for accidents that occur on the property.

Loan-to-Value Ratio (LTV):
A lending risk assessment ratio that lenders examine before approving a mortgage, calculated by dividing the mortgage amount by the appraised property value.

Mortgage:
A loan used to purchase a home, where the property itself serves as collateral until the loan is paid off.

Pre-Approval:
A preliminary evaluation by a lender to determine how much money a potential borrower is eligible to borrow for a mortgage.

Principal:
The amount of money borrowed to buy a home, or the amount of the loan that has not yet been repaid, excluding interest.

Private Mortgage Insurance **(PMI):**
Insurance required by lenders when the down payment is less than 20% of the home's purchase price, protecting the lender if the borrower defaults on the loan.

Title:
A legal document evidencing a person's right to ownership of a property.

Title Insurance:
Insurance that protects the buyer and lender against loss due to disputes over property ownership.

LISA CARR
LICENSED REAL ESTATE AGENT
FLORIDA

www.ingramcontent.com/pod-product-compliance
Lightning Source LLC
Chambersburg PA
CBHW062126220526
45471CB00010B/3902